Wild World

Watching
Sharks
in the Oceans

L. Patricia Kite

www.heinemann.co.uk/library
Visit our website to find out more information about Heinemann Library books.

To order:

☎ Phone 44 (0) 1865 888066

▤ Send a fax to 44 (0) 1865 314091

▣ Visit the Heinemann Bookshop at www.heinemann.co.uk/library to browse our catalogue and order online.

First published in Great Britain by Heinemann Library, Halley Court, Jordan Hill, Oxford OX2 8EJ, part of Harcourt Education. Heinemann is a registered trademark of Harcourt Education Ltd.

© Harcourt Education Ltd 2006
First published in paperback in 2007
The moral right of the proprietor has been asserted.

Editorial: Nancy Dickmann and Sarah Chappelow
Design: Ron Kamen and edesign
Illustrations: Martin Sanders
Picture Research: Maria Joannou and Christine Martin
Production: Camilla Crask
Originated by Modern Age
Printed and bound in Italy by Printer Trento srl

13 digit ISBN 978 0 431 19086 0 (HB)
10 digit ISBN 0 431 19086 0 (HB)

British Library Cataloguing in Publication Data
Kite, L. Patricia
Watching sharks in the oceans. - (Wild world)
597.3
A full catalogue record for this book is available from the British Library.

Acknowledgments
The author and publisher are grateful to the following for permission to reproduce copyright material: Ardea pp. **8** (Douglas David Seifert), **10** (Ralf Kiefner), **17** (Ralf Kiefner), **24** (Douglas David Seifert), **27** (Ron and Valerie Taylor); FLPA pp. **4** (Mike Parry/Minden Pictures), **5** (Fred Bavendam/Minden Pictures), **9** (D.P. Wilson), **14** (Jurgen Christin Sohns), **18** (Tui de Roy/Minden Pictures), **25** (Fred Bavendam/Minden Pictures); Nature Picture Library pp. **11** (Brandon Cole), **16**, **20** (Brandon Cole); Oxford Scientific Films pp. **7**, **22** (Richard Packwood); Sea Images, Inc. p. **26** (Carl Roessler); Seapics pp. **12**, **13**, **15**, **19**, **21**, **23**, **28**, **29** top, **29** bottom. Cover photograph of a shark reproduced with permission of Corbis (Denis Scott).

Dedicated to Daniel and Samuel Raney.

The publishers would like to thank Michael Bright of the BBC Natural History Unit for his assistance in the preparation of this book.

Contents

Words written in bold, **like this**, are explained in the glossary.

Meet the sharks

This is the ocean, the home of sharks. Sharks are fish that come in many different sizes. They can be as short as a pencil or bigger than a school bus.

▲ *The great white shark shares the ocean with many other animals.*

▲ *There are more than 400 kinds of sharks. This is a hammerhead.*

The great white shark is the biggest meat-eating shark. An adult may be as long as a truck. It can weigh more than a large car.

At home in the oceans

Oceans cover more than half of the
Earth's **surface**. From above, the water
looks blue. But the light does not reach
very far into the ocean.

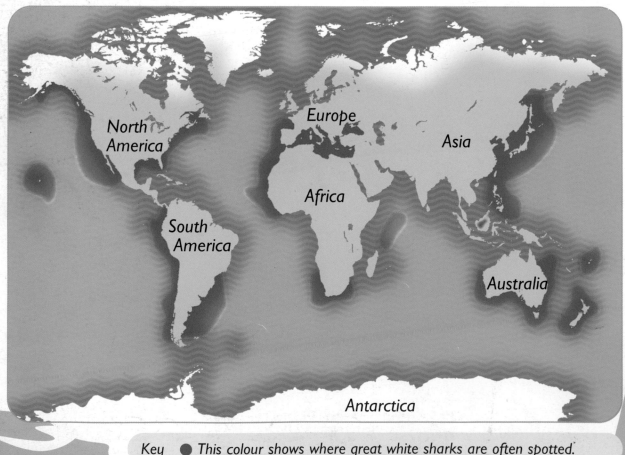

North
America

Europe

Asia

Africa

South
America

Australia

Antarctica

Key ● *This colour shows where great white sharks are often spotted.*

Below the surface, oceans are full of life.
The plants and animals are specially made
for living under water. Great white sharks
are found in deep and **shallow** water.

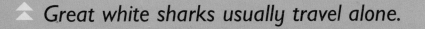
Great white sharks usually travel alone.

There's a shark!

Great white sharks are big, but they are hard to spot. Their backs and sides are grey, and their bellies are white. They blend in from above and below.

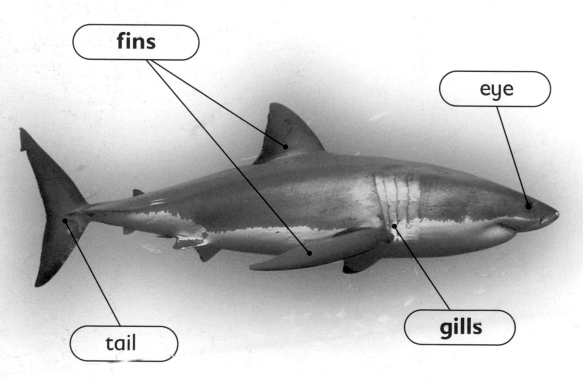

fins

eye

tail

gills

⬆ *From the side, you can see both colours.*

Most fish are covered with smooth **scales**. A shark's body is covered with tiny toothlike prickles. Its skin feels rough, like sandpaper.

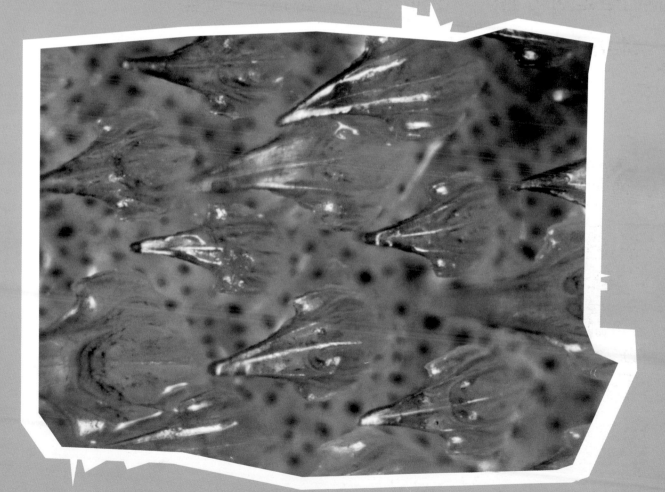

The prickles are called skin teeth or denticles.

Living underwater

Like all animals, sharks need to breathe. They get **oxygen** from the water around them. As the shark swims, water passes over its **gills**.

gills

⏫ *Gills help oxygen move from the water into a shark's blood.*

To get oxygen, sharks must keep water flowing over their gills. Most kinds do this by swimming. If a great white shark stops swimming, it will not get any oxygen.

⏫ *Only a shark's dorsal **fin** can be seen above the surface.*

On the move

A great white shark is built for swimming. It has a smooth body that can glide through the water. A powerful tail pushes it along.

▲ *A shark moves its tail back and forth to swim.*

Sharks can only swim forwards.
They cannot swim backwards.

fins

A shark has **fins** on its back and sides.
They help it balance. When a shark swims
near the **surface**, you might see a fin
above the water.

Shark feast

Great white sharks eat large sea animals. They hunt fish, whales, dolphins, penguins, and other sharks. They also eat dead animals that they find.

▼ *Great white sharks also hunt seals and sea lions.*

A great white shark can kill its prey in one bite.

The shark grabs its **prey** with its lower teeth. It uses its sharp upper teeth to tear it apart. The shark does not chew its food. It swallows it in big chunks.

Shark teeth

A great white shark's mouth is as big as an oven door. There are many rows of teeth, one behind the other. The front row has about 50 sharp teeth.

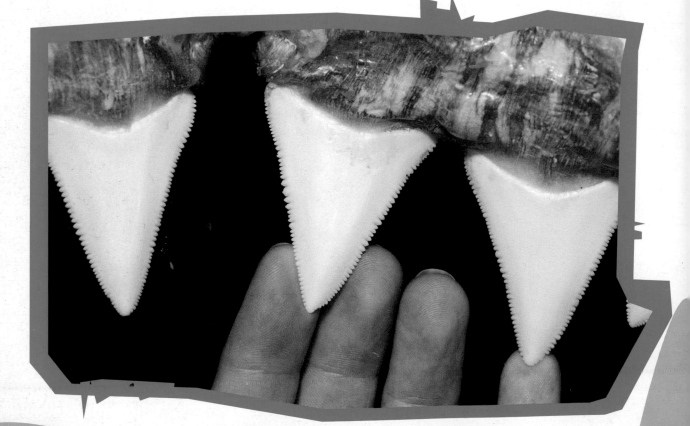

⏶ *Some shark teeth are as big as an egg.*

Shark teeth can break or wear out. When a shark loses a tooth, another moves forward to replace it. This can happen many times.

▲ *A great white shark may go through thousands of teeth in its life.*

Finding food

Sharks cruise slowly through the ocean, looking for food. They have a good **sense** of smell. They sniff for blood or **urine** in the water.

⏶ *A great white shark can smell even one drop of blood.*

Small holes on a shark's side help it find **prey**. The shark also has tiny **organs** in its head. They can **sense** a prey animal's heartbeat.

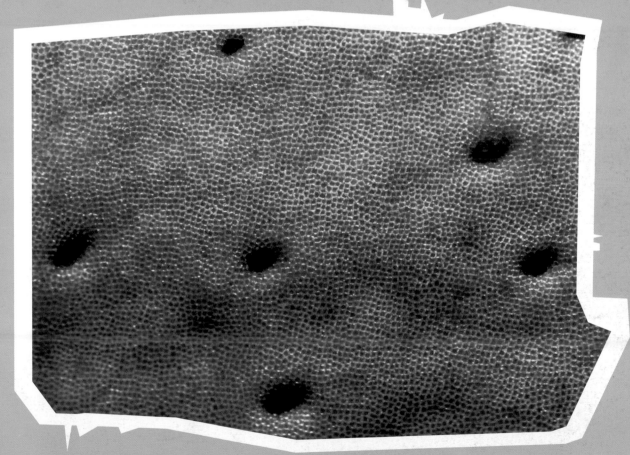

▲ *These holes in a shark's skin can sense the movement of a swimming animal.*

Shark attack!

Once it gets close, the shark uses its eyes to find its target. It attacks from below. **Prey** animals cannot see the shark's grey shape against the dark water.

⏶ *The shark's eyes can spot a seal at the water's **surface**.*

Sometimes the shark leaps out of the water to catch its prey.

The shark swims quickly up towards its prey. When it gets close enough, it opens its mouth and grabs its prey.

From here to there

Great white sharks often stay in one large area. But sometimes they travel a long way. **Scientists** found a shark that swam from California, USA to Hawaii!

▲ *Many great white sharks stay near the **coast**.*

Scientists try to track where great white sharks go. They put a special **tag** on a shark's **fin**. The tag tells the scientist where the shark is.

⏶ *This tag will send information to the scientists' computers.*

Birth and pups

Nobody knows how great white sharks **mate**. A female can give birth to up to 14 babies. After giving birth, she swims away.

▲ **Scientists** *watch great white sharks to find out more about them.*

Baby sharks are called pups. They are as big as a young child. The pups look like their parents. They can swim and hunt straight away.

🔺 Young great white sharks might eat other sharks, like this leopard shark.

Shark enemies

Other sharks can kill shark pups. Killer whales can even kill adult great white sharks. But people are their main enemy.

▲ *Many sharks are killed before they are a year old.*

People kill great white sharks to sell their teeth. Great white sharks are also killed for their meat. There may only be about 10,000 left.

▲ *Many great white sharks get caught up in fishing nets.*

Tracker's guide

When you want to watch animals in the wild, you need to find them first. Great white sharks are tricky, because they live under water.

Scientists can use under water microphones to listen for sharks.

▲ Great white sharks can sometimes be
lured with chunks of raw meat.

◀◀ **Scientists** can track
sharks by putting
tags on their **fins**.

Glossary

coast edge of the land, where it meets the ocean

fin flat part of a fish's body that helps it to swim or turn

gill part of a fish's body that takes oxygen from water to help it breathe

mate when male and female animals produce young. "Mate" can also mean the partner that an animal chooses to have babies with.

organ a body part with a special function, or job

oxygen a gas in the air. People and animals need to breathe in oxygen to stay alive.

prey animal that gets caught and eaten by other animals

scale small, flat piece of hard skin that helps cover a fish's body

scientist person who studies the world around us and how it works

sense to be able to feel, see, smell, hear, or taste something

shallow not deep

surface the top or outer layer of something

tag a piece of material used as a mark or label

urine liquid that animals make to get rid of unwanted water

Find out more

Books

Animal Life Cycles, Anita Ganeri (Heinemann Library, 2005)

Oceans, Angela Royston (Heinemann Library, 2005)

Sea Animals, Francine Galko (Heinemann Library, 2003)

Sharks, Patricia Kendell (Raintree, 2003)

Websites

Visit these websites to find out more amazing facts about sharks.

http://www.mbayaq.org/cr/whiteshark.asp

http://www.nationalgeographic.com/kids/creature_feature/0206/sharks.html

http://www.sdnhm.org/kids/sharks/index.html

Disclaimer

All the internet addresses (URLs) given in this book were valid at the time of going to press. However, due to the dynamic nature of the internet, some addresses may have changed, or sites may have ceased to exist since publication. While the author and publishers regret any inconvenience this may cause readers, no responsibility for such changes can be accepted by either the author(s) or the publishers.

Index